Beginning Guitar

Mastering the Keys

by Jack Petersen

1 2 3 4 5 6 7 8 9 0

Visit us on the Web at www.melbay.com — E-mail us at email@melbay.com

Contents

Foreword

There is no mystery about reading music. It is a skill all musicians should develop regardless of the instrument they play. This book is designed to eliminate fears and suspicions which are often associated with learning to read music.

Key

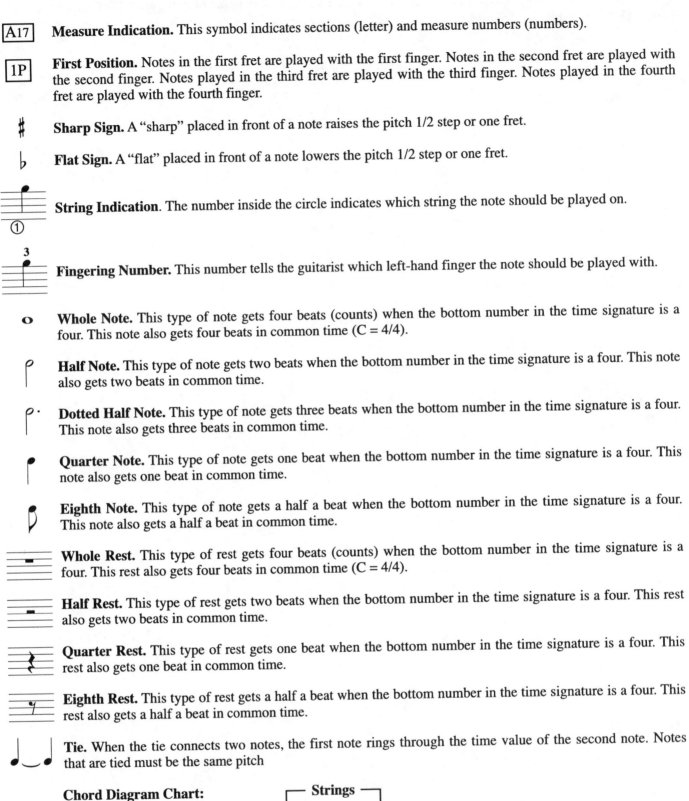

A17   **Measure Indication.** This symbol indicates sections (letter) and measure numbers (numbers).

1P   **First Position.** Notes in the first fret are played with the first finger. Notes in the second fret are played with the second finger. Notes played in the third fret are played with the third finger. Notes played in the fourth fret are played with the fourth finger.

♯   **Sharp Sign.** A "sharp" placed in front of a note raises the pitch 1/2 step or one fret.

♭   **Flat Sign.** A "flat" placed in front of a note lowers the pitch 1/2 step or one fret.

String Indication. The number inside the circle indicates which string the note should be played on.

Fingering Number. This number tells the guitarist which left-hand finger the note should be played with.

Whole Note. This type of note gets four beats (counts) when the bottom number in the time signature is a four. This note also gets four beats in common time (C = 4/4).

Half Note. This type of note gets two beats when the bottom number in the time signature is a four. This note also gets two beats in common time.

Dotted Half Note. This type of note gets three beats when the bottom number in the time signature is a four. This note also gets three beats in common time.

Quarter Note. This type of note gets one beat when the bottom number in the time signature is a four. This note also gets one beat in common time.

Eighth Note. This type of note gets a half a beat when the bottom number in the time signature is a four. This note also gets a half a beat in common time.

Whole Rest. This type of rest gets four beats (counts) when the bottom number in the time signature is a four. This rest also gets four beats in common time (C = 4/4).

Half Rest. This type of rest gets two beats when the bottom number in the time signature is a four. This rest also gets two beats in common time.

Quarter Rest. This type of rest gets one beat when the bottom number in the time signature is a four. This rest also gets one beat in common time.

Eighth Rest. This type of rest gets a half a beat when the bottom number in the time signature is a four. This rest also gets a half a beat in common time.

Tie. When the tie connects two notes, the first note rings through the time value of the second note. Notes that are tied must be the same pitch

Chord Diagram Chart:

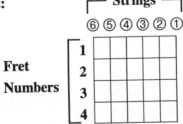

Dynamics. The aspect of musical expression concerned with changes in volume is called "dynamics." Written below are the various symbols and terms written in music to indicate the use of dynamics

SYMBOL	ENGLISH	ITALIAN	FRENCH	GERMAN
fff	Extremely loud	Fortississimo	Trés fort	Äusser laut
ff	Very loud	Fortissimo	Trés fort	Sehr laut
f	Loud	Forte	Fort	Laut
mf	Moderately loud	Mezzo forte	Mi-fort	Halbstark
mp	Moderately soft	Mezzo piano	Mi-doux	Halbleise
p	Soft	Piano	Doux	Leise
pp	Very soft	Pianissimo	Trés doux	Sehr leise
ppp	Extremely soft	Pianississimo	Trés doux	Äusser leise

 Key Signature. The key signature is a set of sharps (♯) or flats (♭) placed at the beginning of a composition between the clef sign and the time signature. It indicates which notes will be sharp or flat throughout the entire piece.

 If there are no sharps or flats at the beginning of the music, the piece is in the key of C major. The first compositions in this book are in the key of C major.

Repeat Signs. This, :‖ , is a repeat sign. Go from this sign to the place where the double bars on the other side appears (‖:). After repeating, skip the first ending ⌐1.⌐ and go on to the second ending ⌐2.⌐ .

2X Skip 1st end, play 2nd ending & continue

When reaching the part where a "*D.C. al Coda*" is written, (D.C. stands for Da Capo and indicates to go to the beginning) play from the beginning of the piece until the sign *To Coda* ⊕. Go from this point to the sign ⊕*Coda* near the end of the piece. Then, play to the end. The coda is the final added section of the piece.

D.C. al Coda: Go back to the top, play until Coda, and jump to Coda

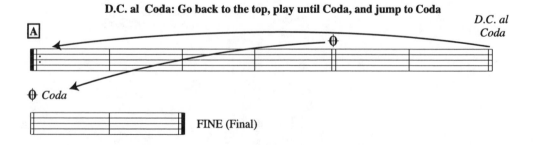

When the phrase "*D.S.* 𝄌 *al Coda*" or "*D.S.* 𝄌 *al Fine*" appears at the end of a piece, go back to the sign 𝄌 and play until you reach the **Coda** or the word **Fine**, which means "The End."

D.S. 𝄌 al Fine: Go back to 𝄌, play until Fine

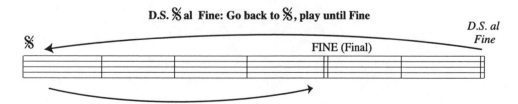

Each **major key** has a **relative minor key**. Both scales have the same key signature. The first note of the relative minor scale will begin on the sixth note of the major scale. As shown below, A minor is the relative minor to C major.

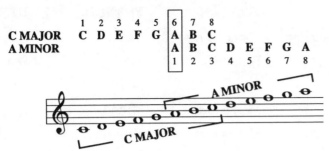

Guidelines for Reading Music The following list shows considerations to make when reading music. Check:

a. Tempo
b. Key Signature
c. Time Signature
d. Range
e. Directions
f. Dynamics
g. Forms (various sections in the music)

Guitar Parts

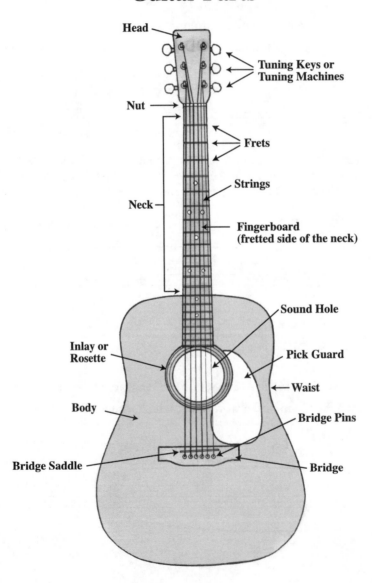

Scooter

In section A, the tonality is C major. In section B, the tonality is A minor. These are relative keys, which means they have the same key signature. While these keys have the same key signature, they do not have the same sound.

Straight 8's

MM ♩ = 138

Blues

Blues is a very important part of American music. Blues is 12 bars (measures) in length and is comprised of 3, four-bar phrases:

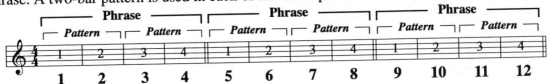

A "sequence" is the repetition of a short musical phrase. "Pattern" is another word for sequence. Patterns are used within a phrase. A two-bar pattern is used in each of the blues phrases.

The use of three, four-bar phrases is constant throughout all four blues etudes which follow.

Blues Pattern #1

Lonesome Cowboy

This etude introduces a **tie** (♩‿♩). A tie creates longer duration on a note across the bar line. A curved line is used to indicate a tie.

Accidentals

When the sharp sign appears in front of a note, raise the note 1/2 step (one fret). When the flat sign appears in front of a note, lower the note 1/2 step (one fret). To flat an open string, go to the next largest string and place the finger in the fret to match the open string. Then, flat the note by moving it down one fret. A natural sign (♮) cancels a sharp or flat. Sharp, flat, and natural signs are called "accidentals."

An accidental is only valid within the measure it is written. In the next measure, the accidental is canceled and the note returns to its original pitch. Accidentals effect all the same notes which follow in the measure, unless a natural sign is written. A natural cancels a sharp or flat.

Claudette's Theme

The composition *Claudette's Theme* is written in C major and A minor. Sections A and A9 are in C major. Sections B and B9 are in A minor. In section B9, there is a G sharp which is played on the third string, first fret.

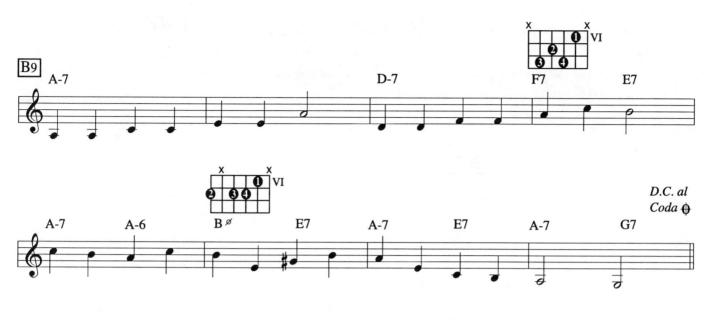

B9 A-7　　　　　　　　　　　　　　　　D-7　　　　　　　　　F7　　　　E7

A-7　　　A-6　　　Bø　　E7　　A-7　　E7　　A-7　　G7

D.C. al
Coda ⊕

⊕

C　　　　Fine

Exercises in the Key of F Major

The following are short exercises in the key of F major. The B♭ is in the key signature and it shows in brackets throughout. The etudes have only the key signatures.

Ex. #1

Ex. #2

Ex. #3

Ex. #4

Haze

This etude is in F major and D minor (relative minor of F major).
Letters A and A9 are in F major. Letters B and B9 are in D minor.
Listen for repetition of themes at the beginning of each letter.

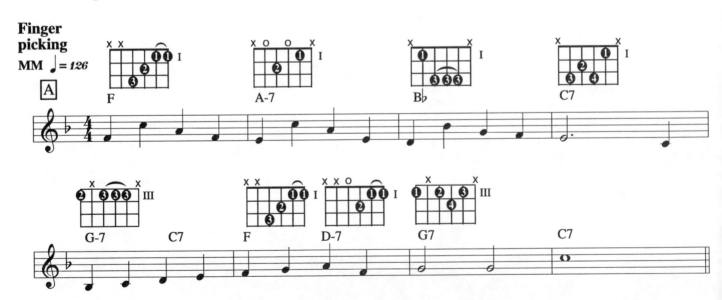

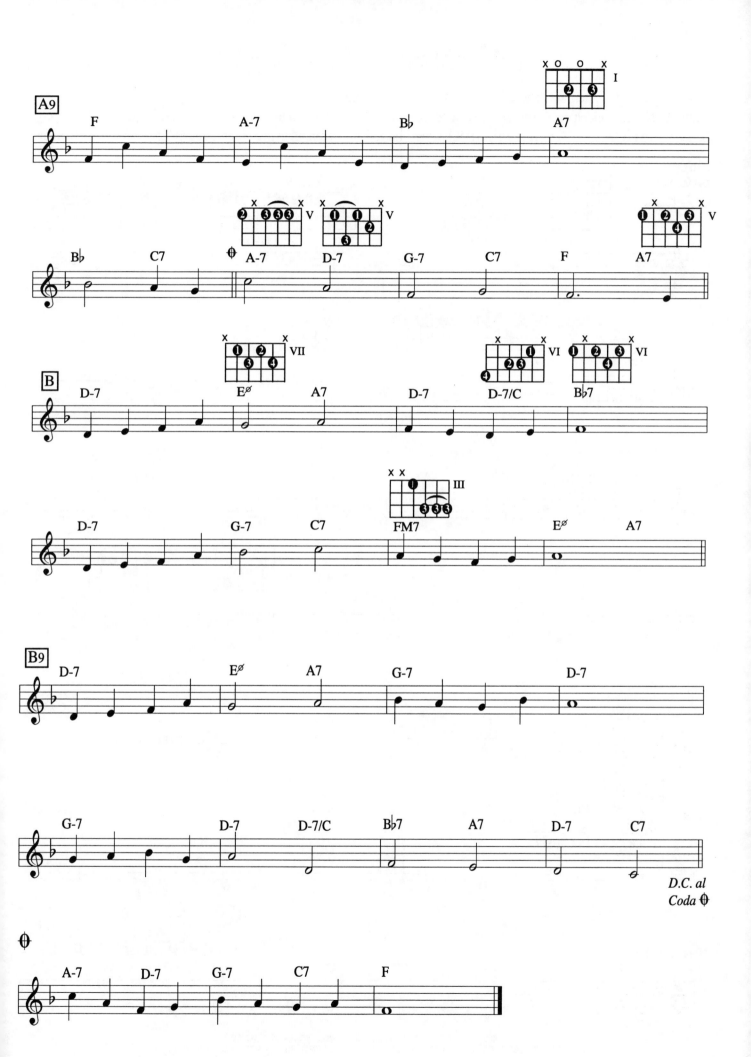

October Twilight

Letters [A] and [A9] alternate between F major and D minor within each letter.
Letter [B] has an accidental. B natural is indicated instead of B flat. Relate letter B to the key of C major.
Letter [C] is a **tag**. A tag is like a post script (P.S.), when you add an after thought in a letter. Letter [C] is an after thought in music.

Scamp the Cat

This etude is in D minor. There are several accidentals throughout. Letters A and A9 have accidentals in the second and sixth bars. Letter A17 has accidentals in bars one, two, five and six.
Letter A25 is the same as A except for the last two bars.

Exercises in the Key of B♭ Major

The following are short exercises in the key of B♭ major. The B♭ and E♭ are in the key signature and in brackets throughout. The etudes have only the key signatures.

Ex. #1

Ex. #2

Ex. #3

Ex. #4

Pretty Katie

This etude is in the key of B♭ major. Letter A has a first and second ending. Letter A17 is what is called a **bridge**, Letter A25 is the same as letter A with the second ending.

Fine

Buster's Bounce

This etude is in the key of G minor which is the relative minor of B♭ major. There are three accidentals in this piece. Letter **A** sixth bar. Letter **A17** seventh bar. Letter **A25** sixth bar.

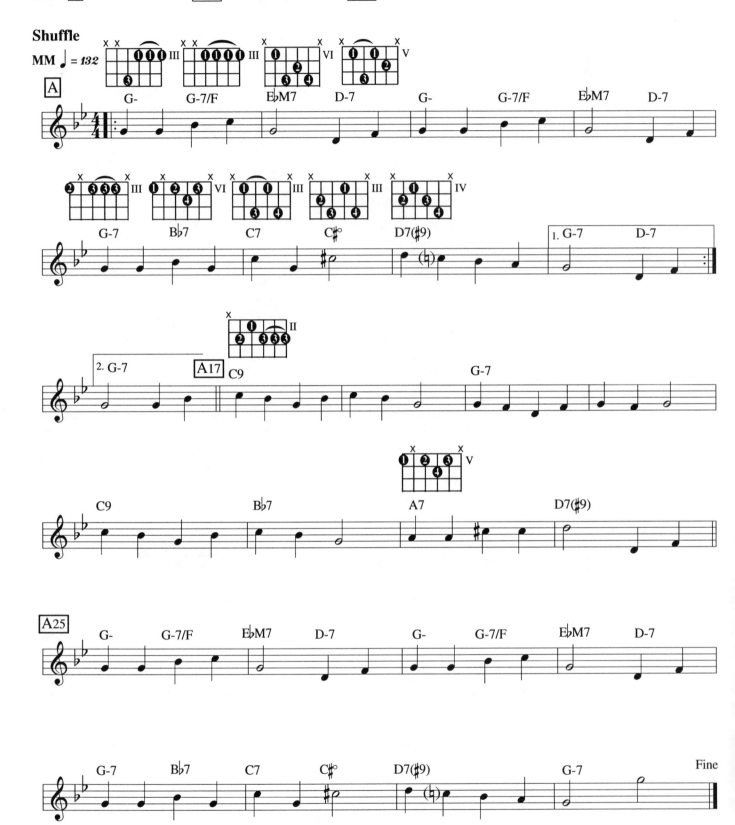

'Till We Meet Again

This etude introduces an enharmonic note. An enharmonic note is one that has two different names but sounds the same. For example:

The reason for this is if the music is ascending, sharps or naturals are used. If the music is descending, flats or naturals are used. For example:

This etude is in Bb major throughout. Letter [A] has accidentals in bars one, five. six, and eight. Letter [A9] has accidentals in bars three, five and eight. Letter [A17] has accidentals in bars one, five and six. Letter [A25] has accidentals in bars 1 and 5. A quarter rest is in bar 8th in both, [A9] , and [A17]. To **rest** in music means **silence** or **do not play**.

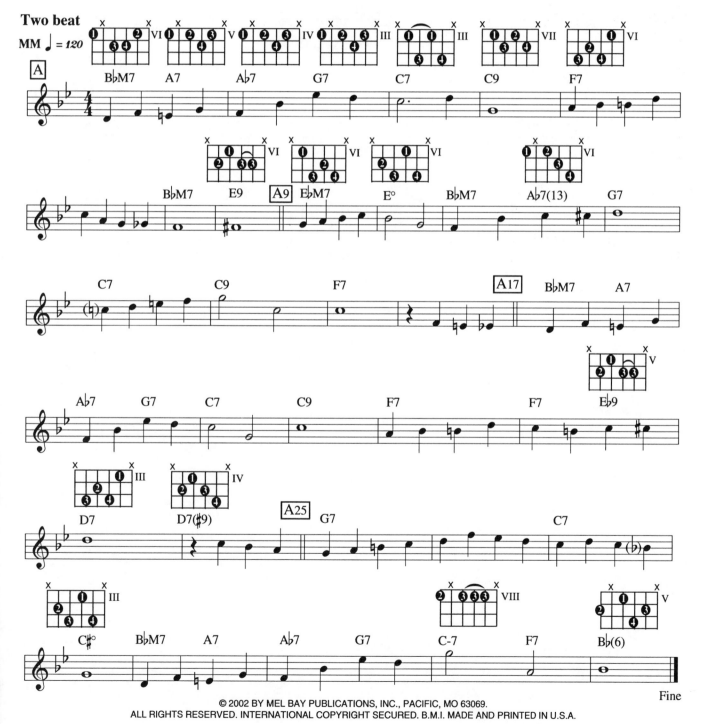

Exercises in the Key of E♭ Major

The following are short exercises in the key of E♭ major. The B♭, E♭ and A♭ are in the key signature and in brackets throughout. The etudes have only the key signatures.

Ex. #1

Ex. #2

Ex. #3

Ex. #4

Secrets

This etude is in the key of E♭ major. The first six bars of both, letter A and A9 are the same.

Marvin's Trip

This etude is in the key of C minor and E♭ major. Letters A and A9 are in C minor with one accidental in bar six. Letter B is in E♭ major with no accidentals.

River Passage

This etude is in the key of E♭ major and C minor. Letters [A] and [A9] are in E♭ major. Letters [B] and [B9] are in C minor with accidentals in bars two and four.

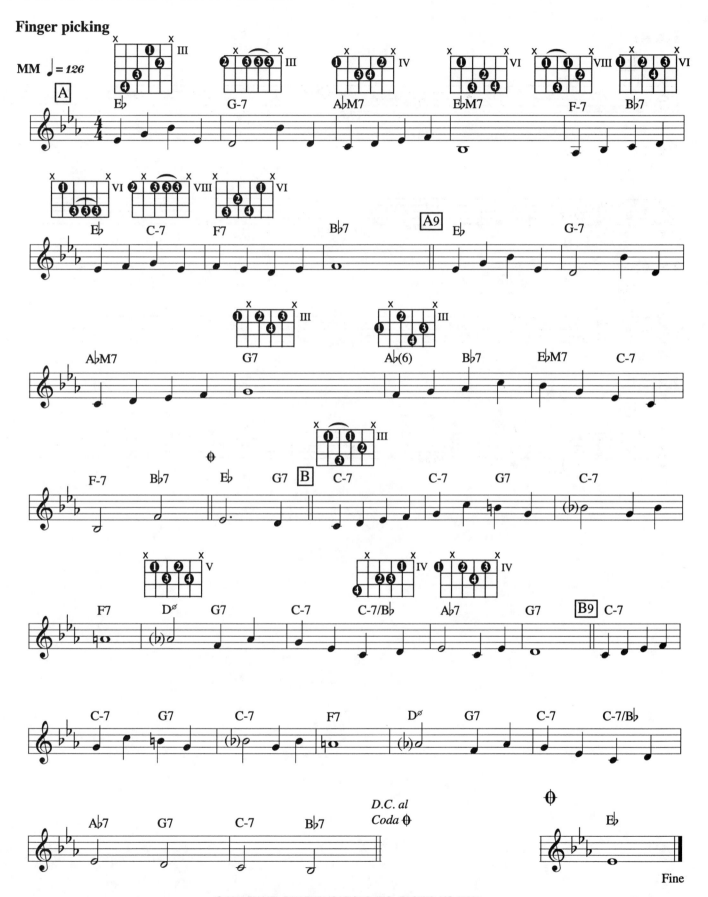

Exercises in the Key of Ab Major

The following are short exercises in the key of Ab major. The Bb, Eb, Ab and Db are in the key signature and in brackets throughout. The etudes have only the key signatures.

Ex. #1

Ex. #2

Ex. #3

Ex. #4

Just for the Fun of It

This etude is in the key of A♭ major.

Bread and Butter

This etude is in the key of F minor and A♭ major. Letter [A] is in the key of F minor. Bar two has two accidentals. Bars three and nine have one accidental each. Letters [B] and [B9] are in the key of A♭ with accidentals in the coda. Within the coda, bars four and five have one accidental each.

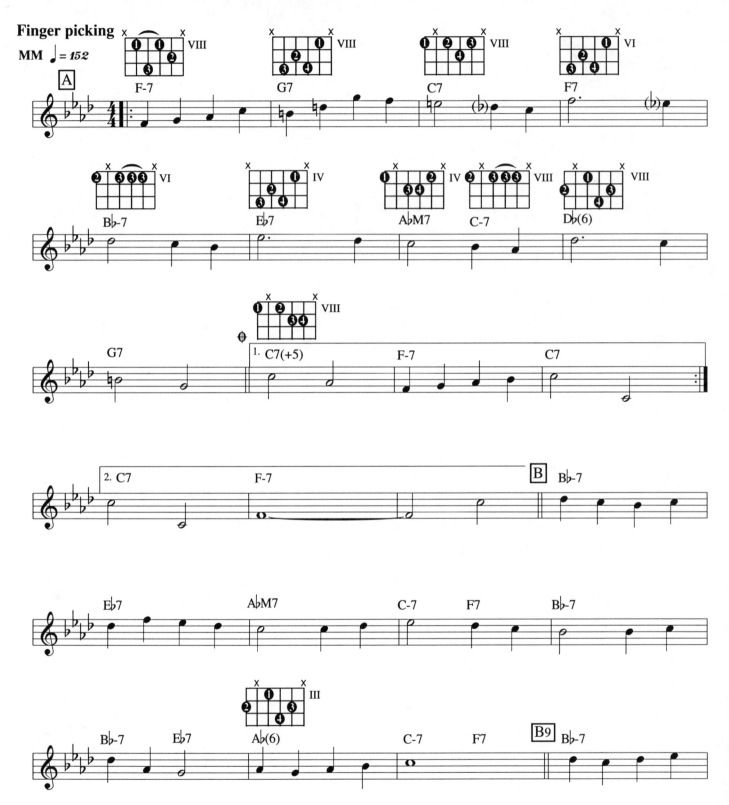

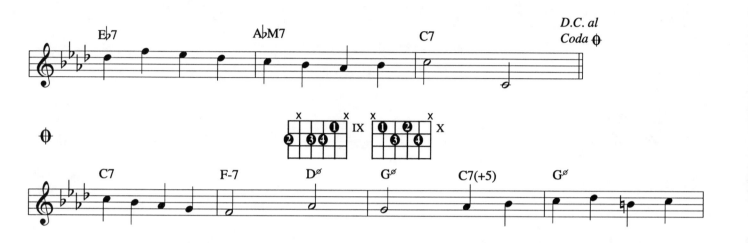

Exercises in the Key of Db Major

The following are short exercises in the key of Db major. The Bb, Eb, Ab, Db and Gb are in the key signature and in brackets throughout. The etudes have only the key signatures.

Ex. #1

Ex. #2

Ex. #3

Ex. #4

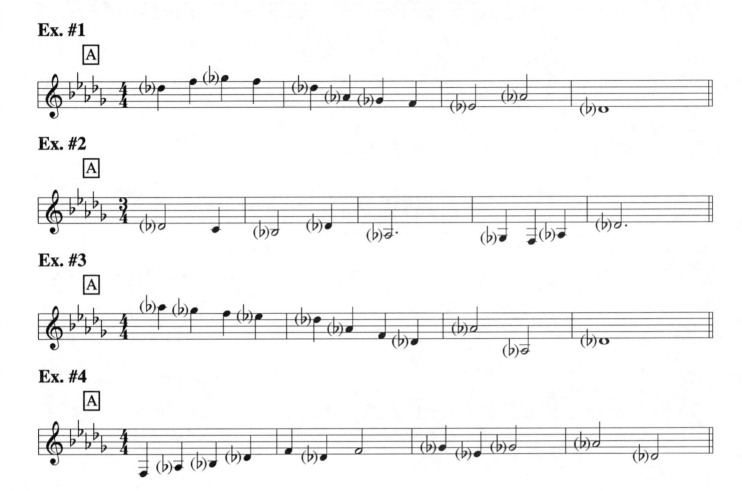

So Long

This etude is in the key of D♭ major. There is a pickup note at the beginning. At the end of letter B is D.C. al Coda.

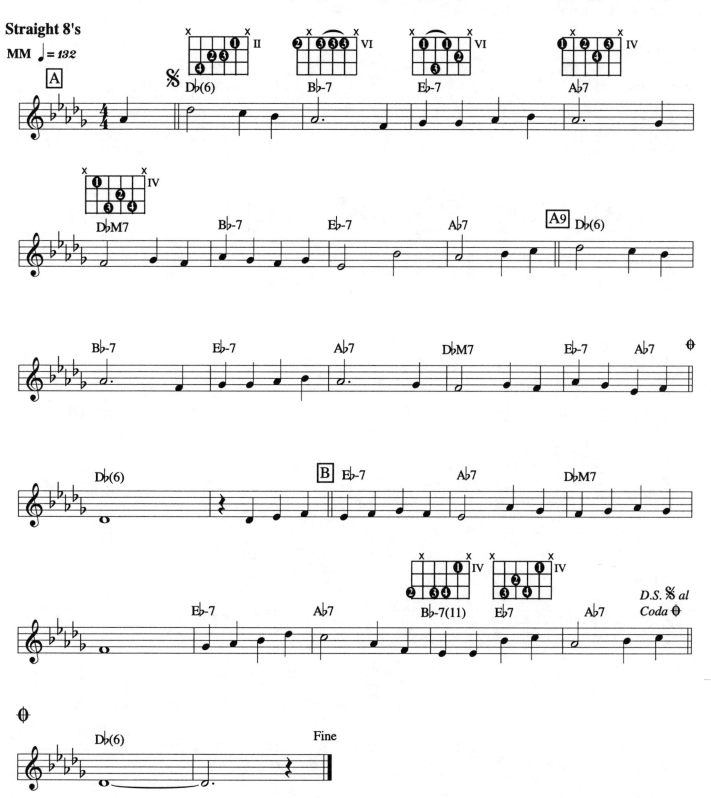

Lonesome

This etude is in the key of B♭minor and D♭ major. Letter [A] and [A9] alternate between B♭minor and D♭ major. Letter [B] stays in B♭minor. At the end of [B] is D.C. al Coda.

Exercises in the Key of G Major

The following are short exercises in the key of G major. The F♯ is in the key signature and in brackets throughout. The etudes have only the key signatures.

Ex. #1

Ex. #2

Ex. #3

Ex. #4

Twinkle

This etude is in 3/4 meter and in the key of G major and E minor.
Letters A and A9 are in G major. Letters B and B9 are in E minor.

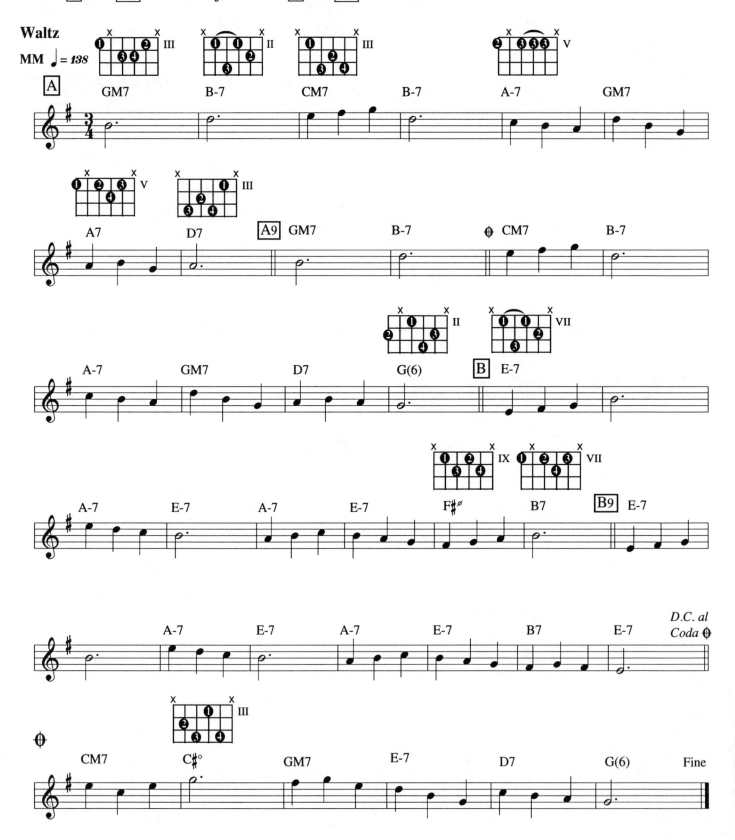

Soft Eyes

This etude is in G major. Letter $\boxed{A}$ has accidentals in bars 2, 6, and 7. Letter $\boxed{A9}$ has one accidental in bar six. Letter $\boxed{A17}$ same as letter $\boxed{A}$.

Finger picking

Mirage

This etude is in G major throughout. Letter A has accidental in bar five. Letter A17 has accidental in bar five. Letter A25 has accidental in bar four. It also has first and second endings.

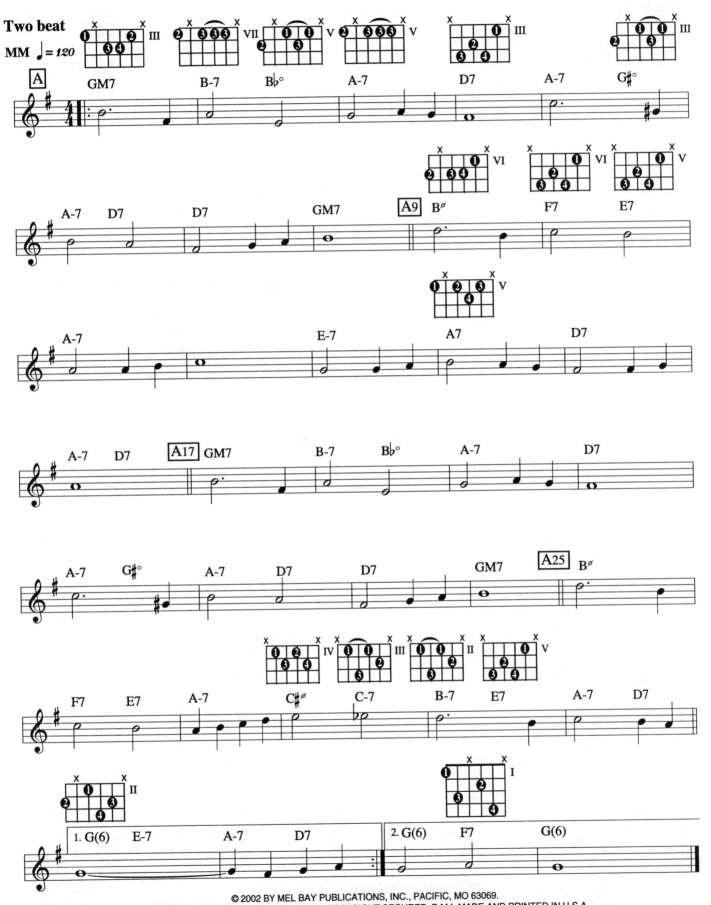

Exercises in the Key of D Major

The following are short exercises in the key of D major. The F♯, and C♯ are in the key signature and in brackets throughout. The etudes have only the key signatures.

Ex. #1

Ex. #2

Ex. #3

Ex. #4

Contrast

This etude is in the key of D major.

Finger picking

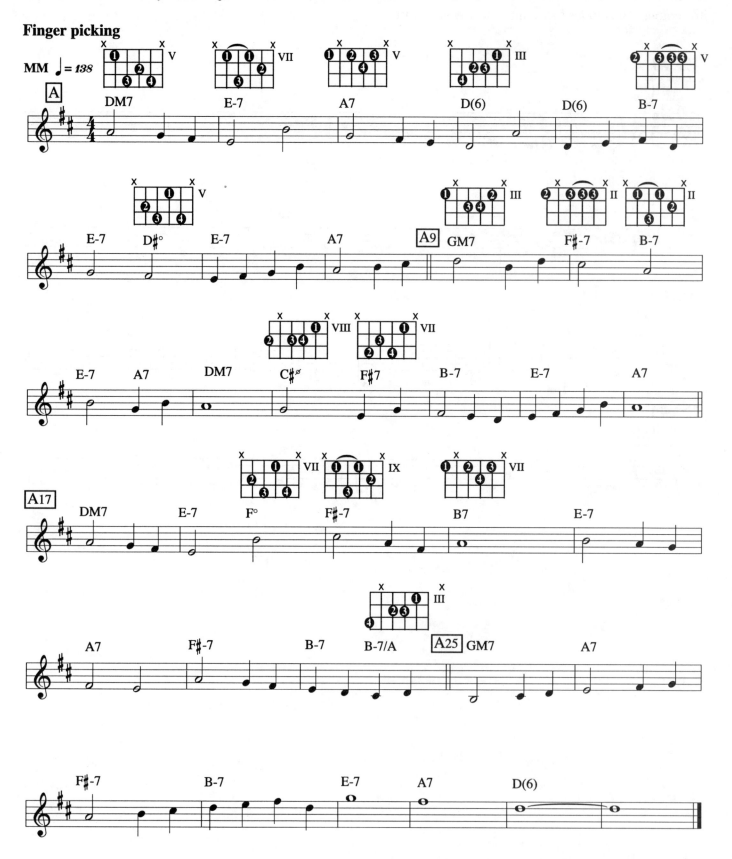

Ester's Lament

This etude is in the key of D major throughout. Letter A has no accidentals. Letter A9 has one accidental in bar five.

Finger picking

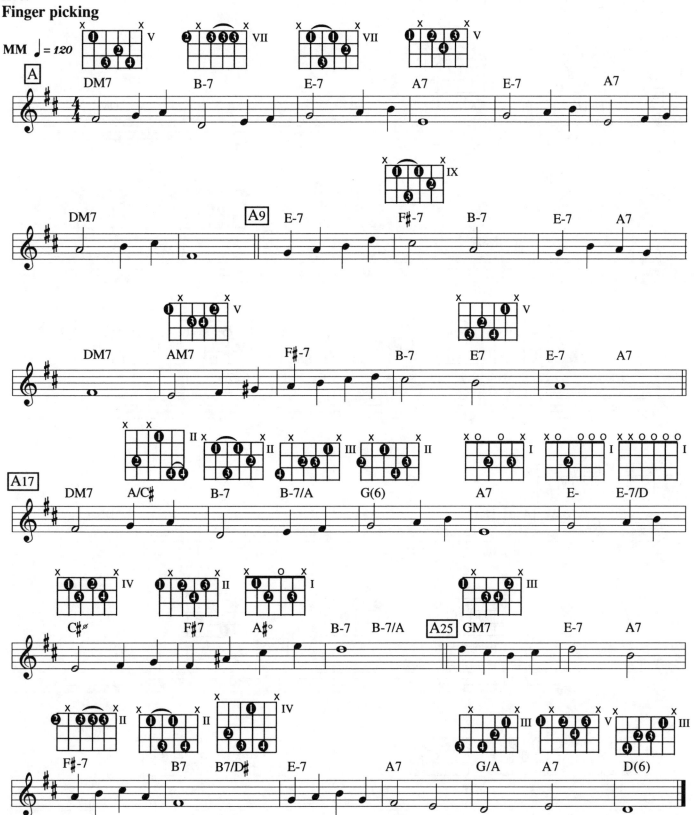

Carefree and Happy

This etude is in D major. Letter [A] has accidentals in bar two, four and six. Letter [A9] has one accidental in bar six. Letter [A17] same as letter [A].

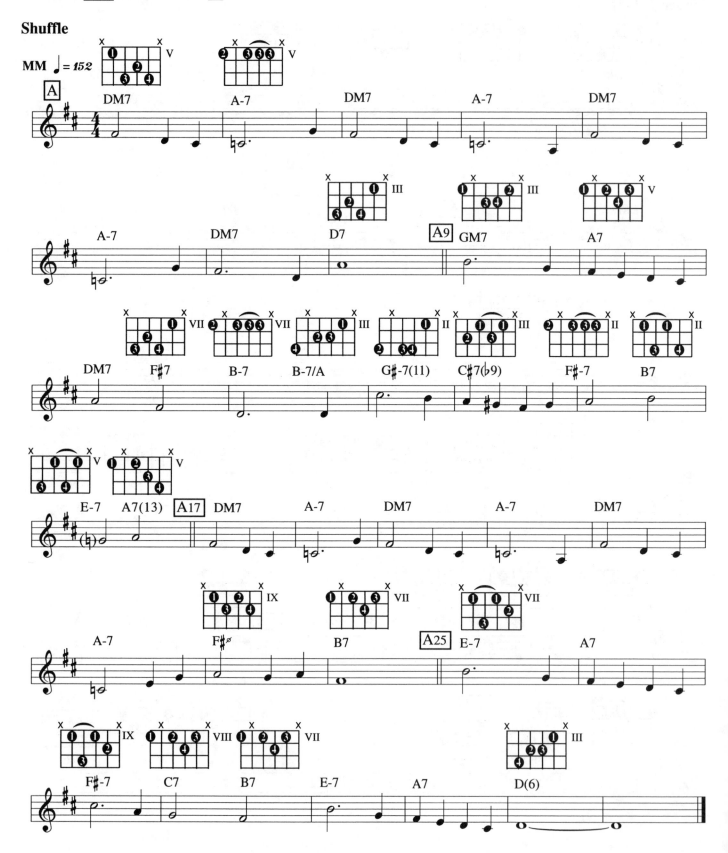

Exercises in the Key of A Major

The following are short exercises in the key of A major. The F♯, C♯, and G♯ are in the key signature and in brackets throughout. The etudes have only the key signatures.

Ex. #1

Ex. #2

Ex. #3

Ex. #4

Sorta Country

This etude has two pickup notes. There are no accidentals. This etude is in A major. Listen for theme repetition.

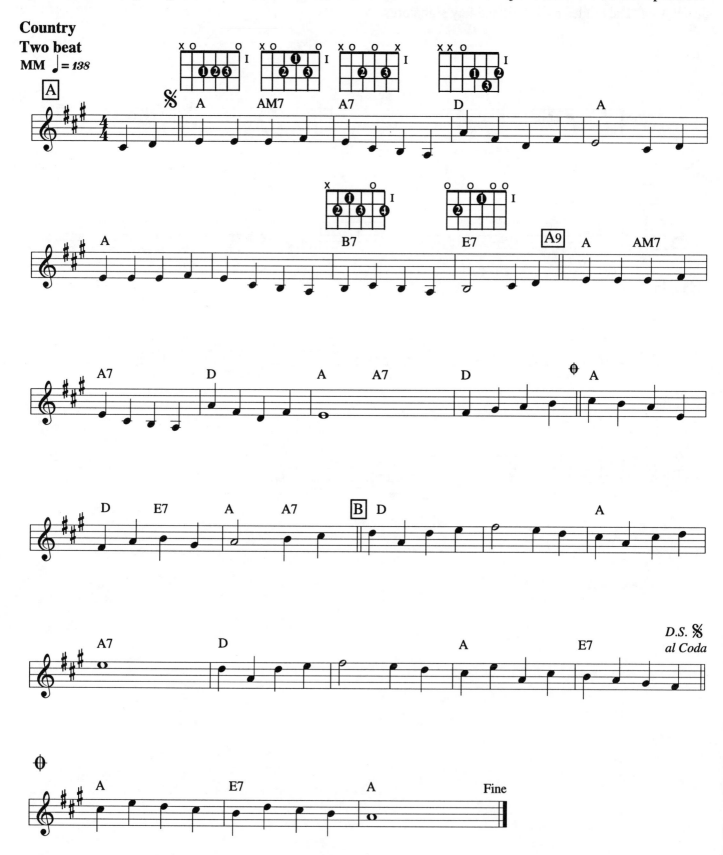

Wings

This etude is in the key of A major and F# minor. Letters [A] and [A9] are in the key of A major. Letter [B] is in the key F# minor. Letter [B9] is F# minor with one accidental in bar three. Letter [C] is in the key of A major with no accidentals. Letter [C9] is A major with one accidental in bar three.

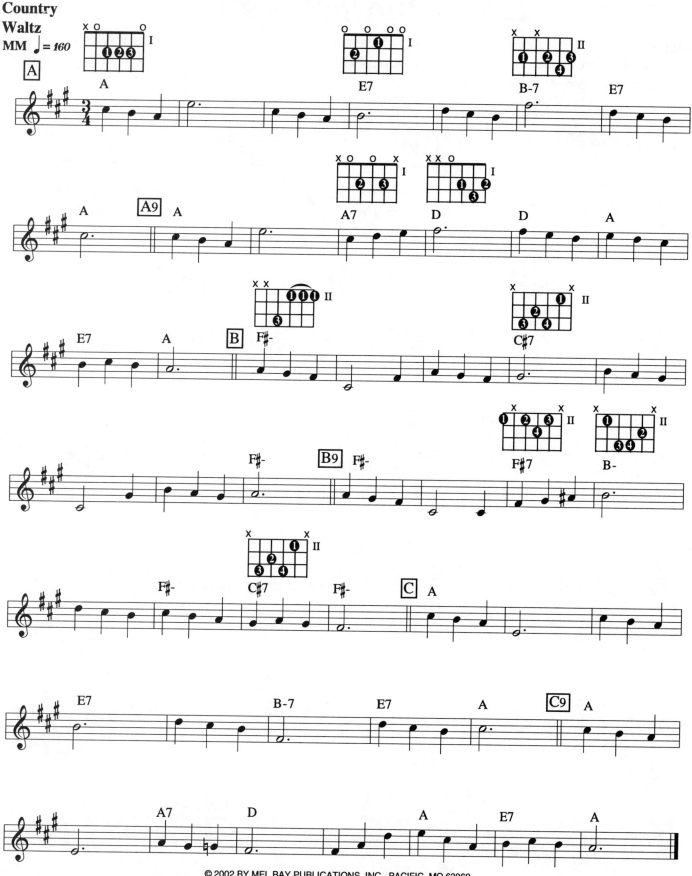

Longer Studies

This section has longer etudes with many accidentals throughout.

Chris and His Gang

This etude alternates between A minor and C major. Listen for repetition and sequences. Letter A9 one accidental in bar five. Letter C three accidentals in bars one, three and five. Letter D9 one accidental in bar five. Letters E and E9 have accidentals in bars five and six.

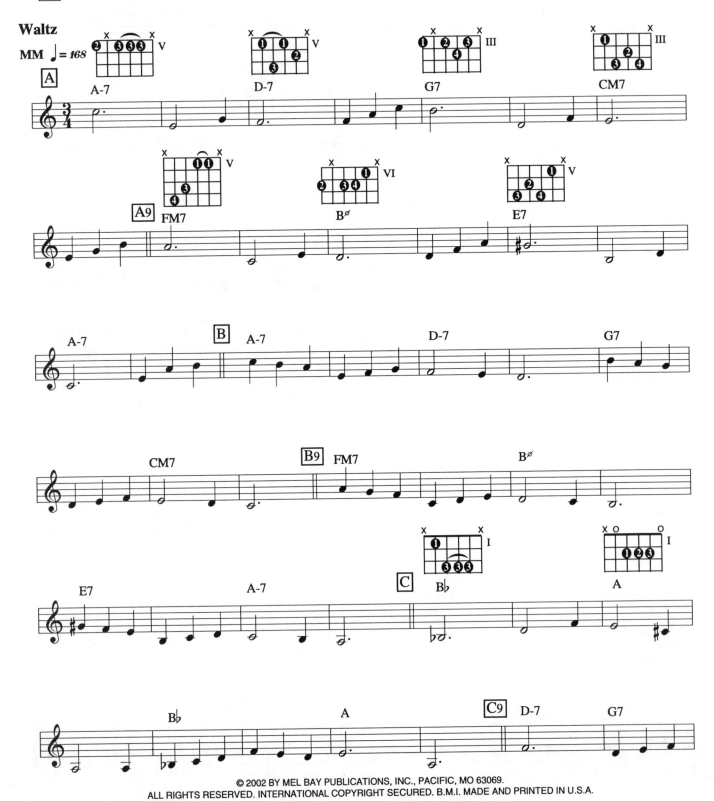

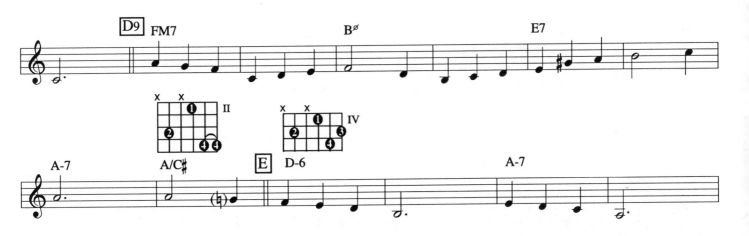

Gee Whiz

This etude is in G major and E minor. Listen for repetition and sequences. Letter $\boxed{A}$ - G major with accidentals in bars one, three and five. Letter $\boxed{A9}$ - same as $\boxed{A}$ only an octave lower. Letter $\boxed{B}$ - E minor with accidentals in bars two, four and seven. Letter $\boxed{B9}$ - E minor with accidentals in bars two and four. Letter $\boxed{C}$ - E minor. Letter $\boxed{C9}$ - E minor with one accidental in bar six.

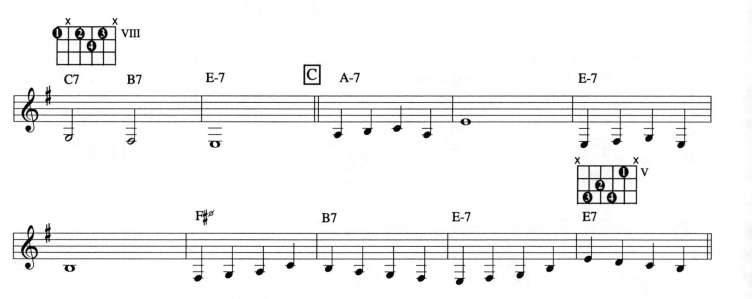

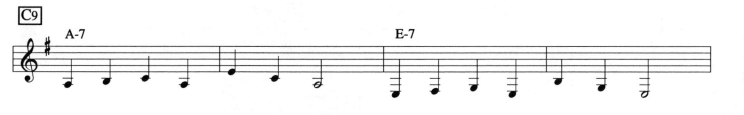

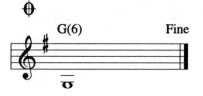

D.C. al
Coda ⊕

⊕
G(6)   Fine

Ode to a Toad

This etude alternates between B minor and D major. Letter A - accidentals in bars two and three. Letter A9 - accidentals in bar eight. Letter B - same as A. Letter C - accidentals in bars four, five and six. Letter C9 - accidentals in bars two and three. CODA - accidental in bar eight.

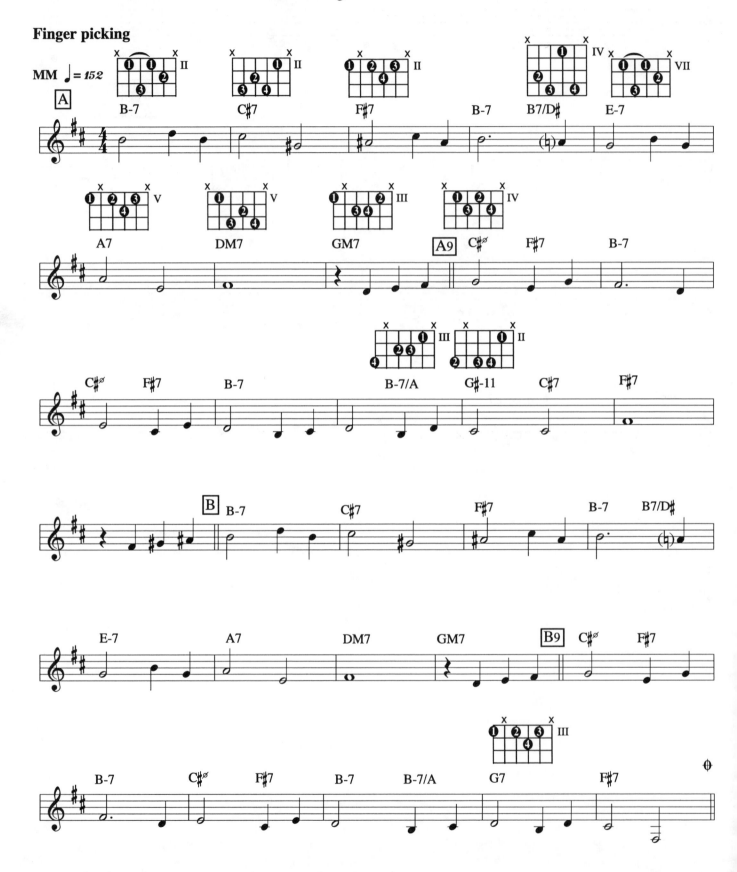

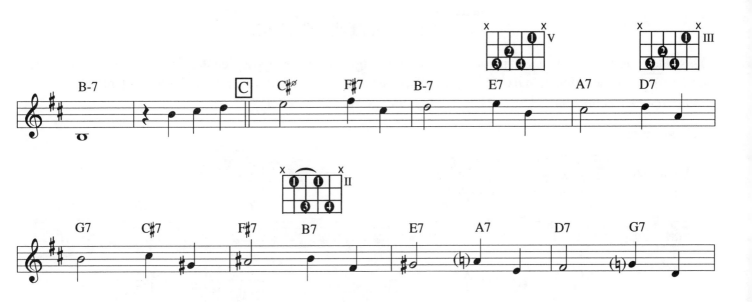

The Sad One

This etude alternates between G major and E minor throughout. Letter A - accidentals in bars two, five and seven. Letter A9 - one accidental in bar four. Letter B - one accidental in bar six . Letter B9 - accidentals in bars six and seven. This etude has a long repeat. First ending goes back to letter A.

Finger picking

Many composers write songs that consist of more than one key. Instead of using a new key signature, they use accidentals. This section will concentrate on how to relate these accidentals to a key center. These accidentals usually occur in the middle section of a song.

My Secret Island

This etude has a pickup note. Letter [A] is in the key of D major with accidentals in bars two, three, five, six and seven. It has a first and second endings. Letter [B] modulates to the key of F major. Letter [B7] is in the key of D major. Letter [C] is in the key of D major with accidentals in bars two, three and seven.

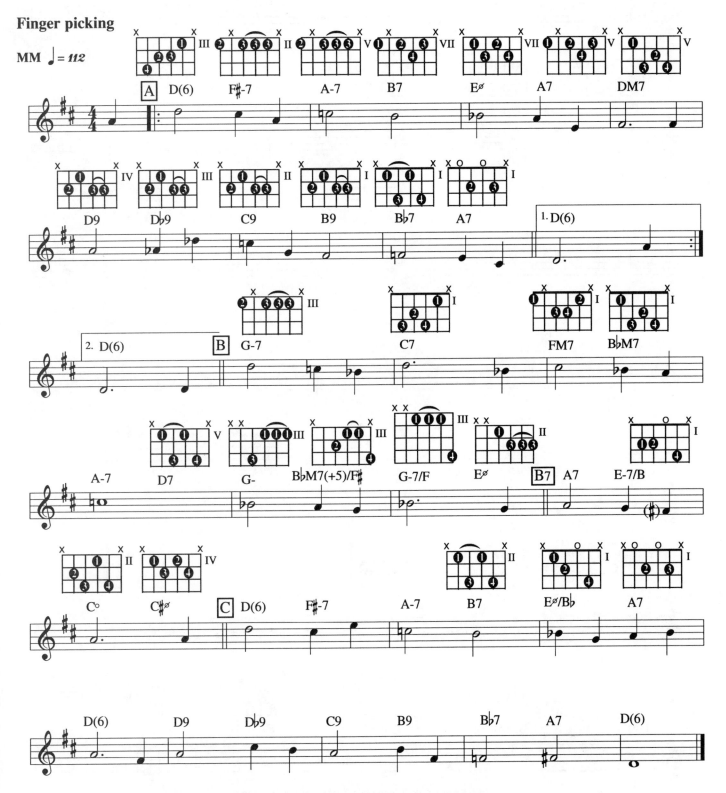

Jill's Waltz

Letter **A** is in the key of F major. Letter **A9** is in the key of F major with one accidental in bar five. Letter **B** modulates to the key of A♭ major. Letter **C** modulates to the key of G major. Bars seven and eight are back in the key of F major.

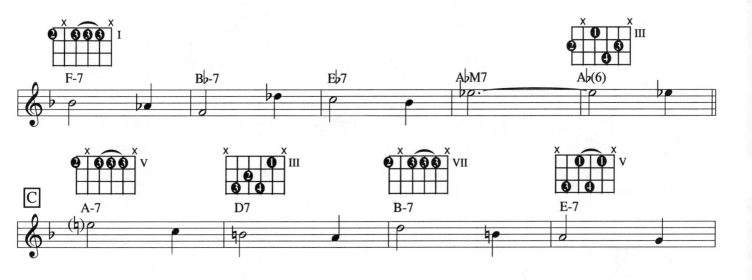

F-7　　　　Bb-7　　　　Eb7　　　　AbM7　　　Ab(6)

C

A-7　　　　D7　　　　B-7　　　　E-7

D.C. al
Coda ⊕

A-7　　　　D7　　　　G-7　　　　C7

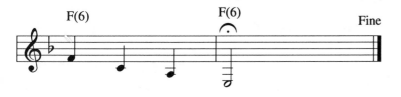

F(6)　　　　F(6)　　　　Fine

Scott's Waltz

Letter A , A9 , and A17 are in the key of B♭ major. Letter A25 is in the key of B♭ major with accidentals in bars one and two. Letter B modulates to the key of D♭ major. Letter C modulates to the key of B♭ minor with accidentals in bar eight.

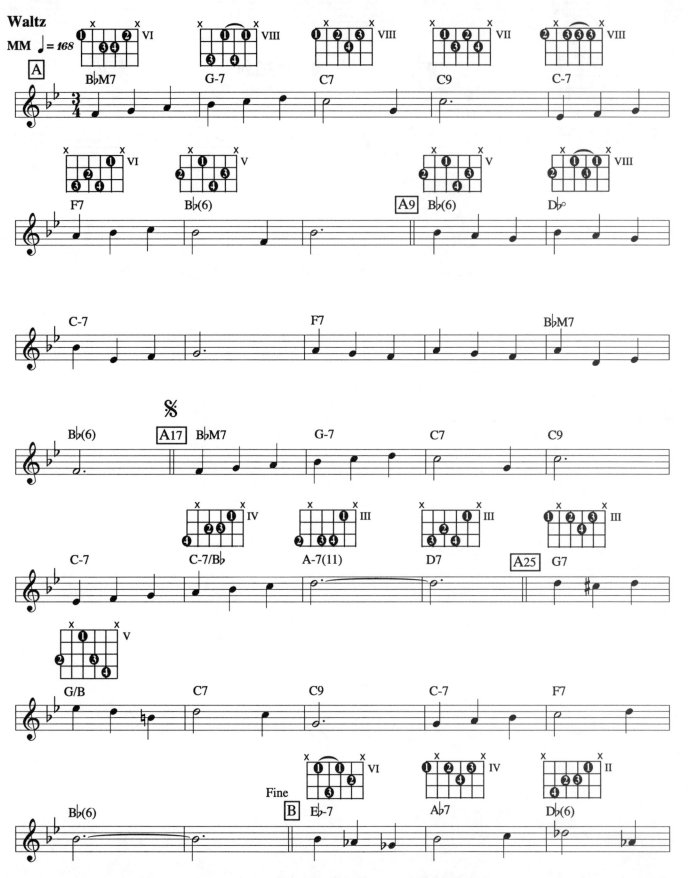

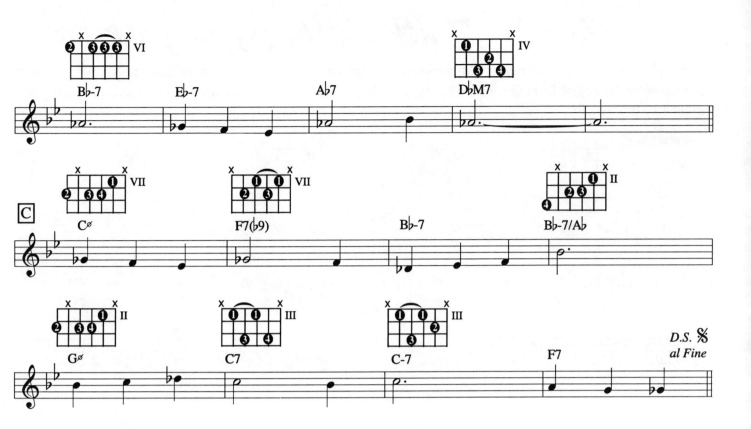

C

D.S. 𝄋
al Fine

Chalk - Talk on the Sidewalk

Letter [A] is in the key of B♭ major with accidental in bar seven. Letter [A9] is in the key of B♭ major. Letter [B] modulates to the key of D♭ major. Letter [C] is in the key of B♭ major with accidentals in bar seven. Letter [C9] is in the key of B♭ major.

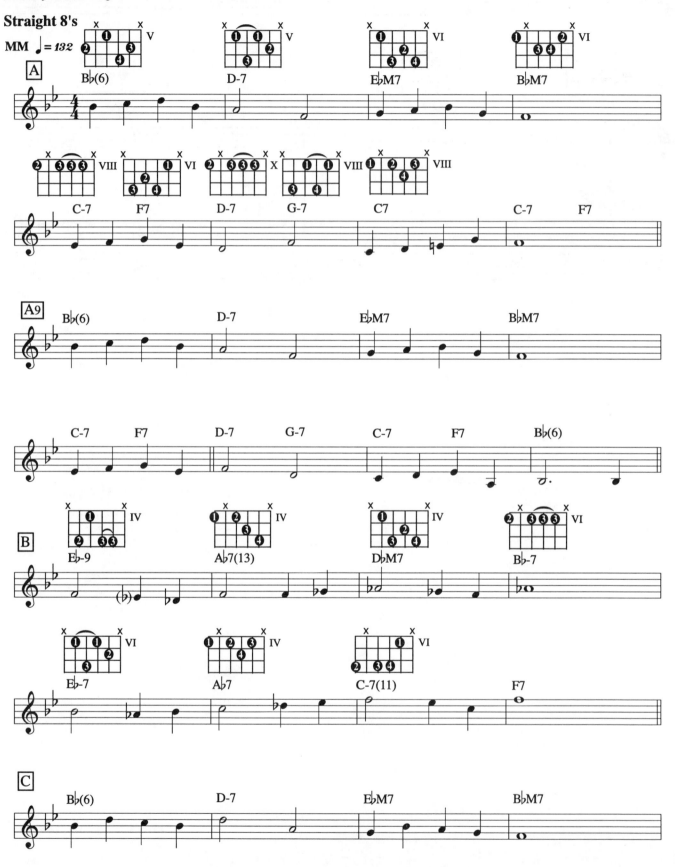

Yesterdays Waltz

Letter $\boxed{A}$ is in the key of D major with an accidental in bar six. Letter $\boxed{A9}$ is in the key of D major, has first and second endings and accidental in the last bar of the second ending. Letters $\boxed{B}$ and $\boxed{B9}$ modulate to the key of B♭ major. Letter $\boxed{B17}$ modulate to the key of B♭ major with accidental in bar five. Letters $\boxed{B25}$ modulate to the key of B♭ major. Letter $\boxed{C}$ is in the key of D major with accidental in bar six. Letter $\boxed{C9}$ is in the key of D major.

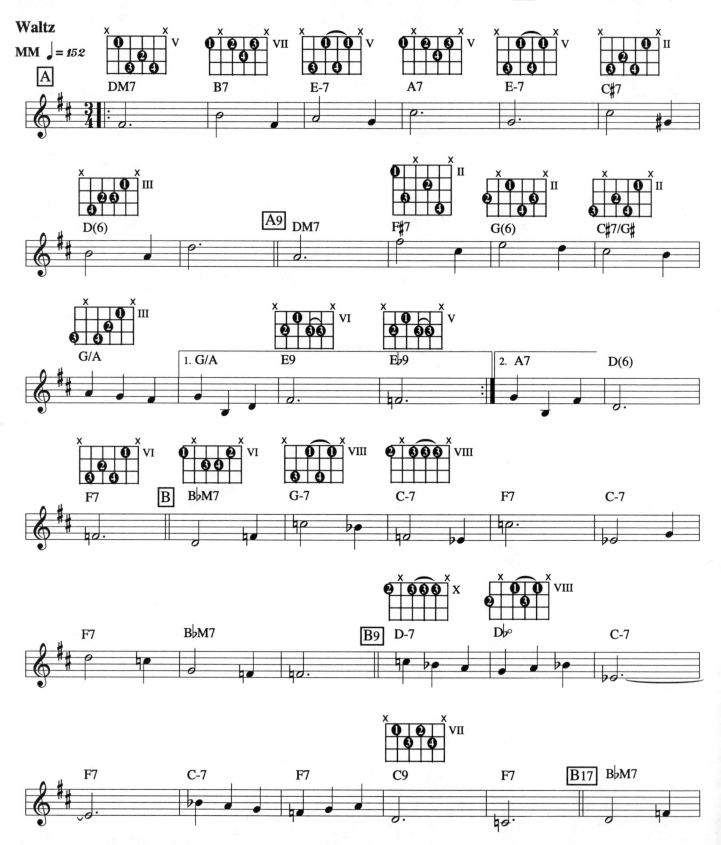

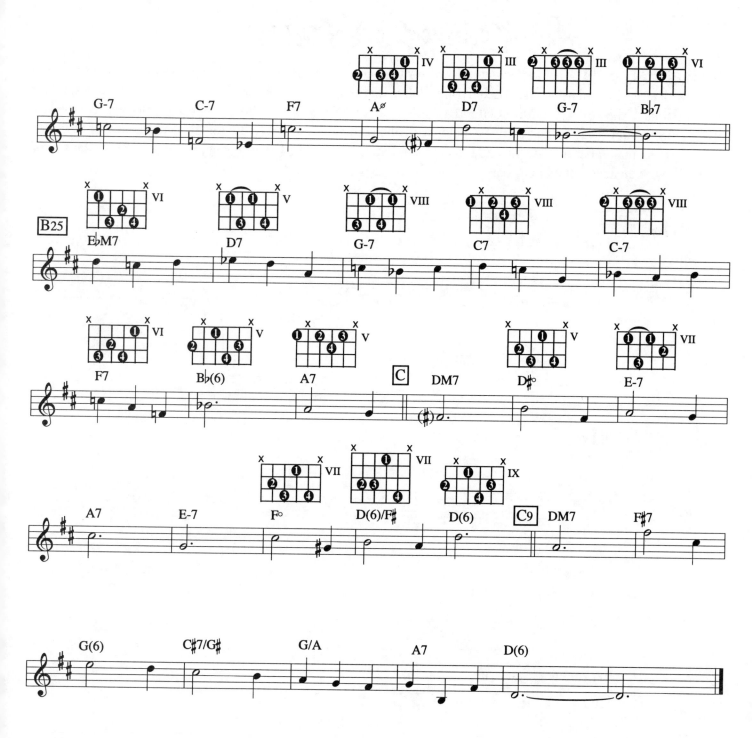

Cheryl's Waltz

Letter A , A9 , and A17 are in the key of E♭ major with an accidental in bar five. Letter A25 is in the key of E♭ major with an accidental in bar eight. Letter B modulates to the key of G major with an accidental in bar eight. Letter B9 modulate to the key of G major. Letter B11 modulate to the key of G minor. Letter B15 modulate to the key of E♭ major. Letter C is in the key of E♭ major with an accidental in bar five. Letter D is in the key of E♭ major with an accidental in bar one. At the end DC al Coda. Letter E is in the key of E♭ major. Letter F is in the key of E♭ major with an accidental in bar one.

Walking on Broadway

Letter $\boxed{A}$ is in the key of A major with accidentals in bars two, four, six and eight. Letter $\boxed{A9}$ is in the key of A major with accidentals in bars two, four, and six. Letter $\boxed{B}$ modulates to the key of C major. Letter $\boxed{C}$ modulates to the key of Bb major. Letter $\boxed{D}$ is in the key of A major.

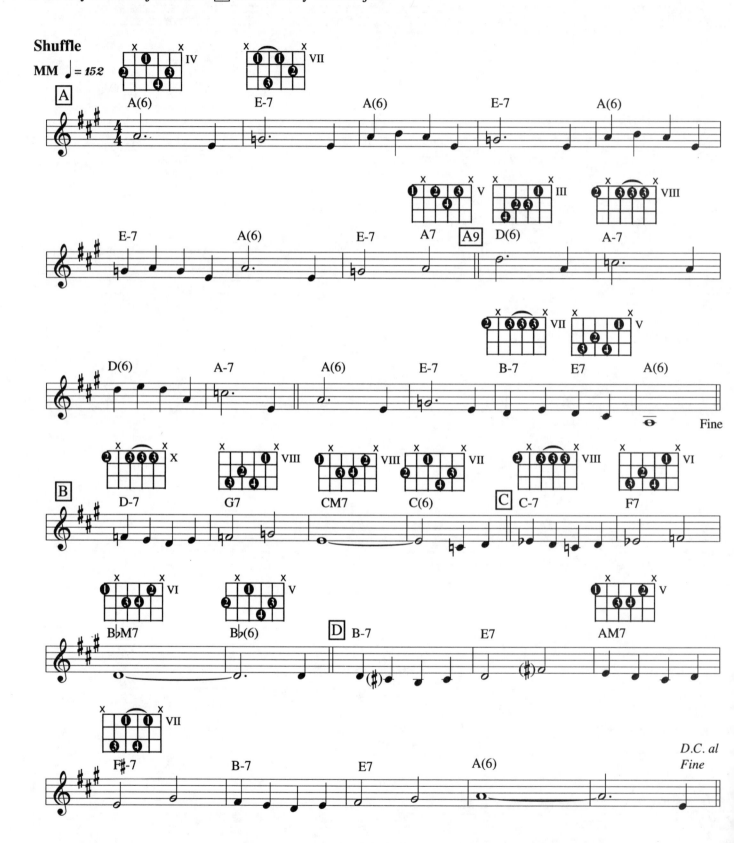